Once Upon a Time...

I Was Never Young

Valorie Tatum

www.weareaps.com

Dedication

I want to thank my mother; my father (who is now deceased); and my siblings. The entangled life of family provided so much information with how to deal with the world.

My mother, now 79, with her untiring love for her children, and being an example of what it means to be a true servant, has inspired me to depths that I didn't even know existed.

Author's Note

This book has been a dream, goal and yearning of mine for a long time. It required a great deal of questioning and reflecting that may or may not agree with the world. However, it is not purposed to judge others; rather, to enlighten about things that plague our thoughts as times, or even consistently.

My life may not be as complicated as others, but we all have things that have aged us in knowledge or behavior far beyond our years. The question is, do we count the experience as weird, special, or just another way of thinking – a different way to see the world?

Sharing my experiences is my way of relaxing and unloading all of the extra thought stored in my head. We are all creatures with flaws, concerns, and unresolved patterns of habit. My hope in sharing this book is that one can say, "I can relate to that", or "I now know why I feel or see things that way", or even, "I no longer have to be afraid of that". I want my readers to recognize and accept that the higher power is a friend indeed, especially in the time of need.

So read with an honest, open mind, heart and spirit. Know that these are my thoughts, experiences and journey and that yours may differ. Know that this is written with observations and reflections intended to help and not offend. Know that all of us have a gift or talent that is useful. If you've not already discovered yours, continue to search for it.

Once upon a time, I was never young…and I have no regrets.

<u>Chapter One</u>

My life became apparent to me when I was five years old. My mother says I always asked questions so that I could solve problems. It was at 5, that my parents purchased and moved us into our new home; I'm 49, and still live in that same home.

The community was unified when it came to raising children, organizing events, and being positive role models. In the last 25+ years, some of those goals, ambitions, and thoughts have seemingly become something of the past.

My thoughts began to reflect back on a morning in 2012 about 12:19 am. I was lying in bed watching Life Today, a spiritual show. This episode was different because the hosts, James and Becky Robinson, were on vacation, so their family members hosted in their stead.

The topic was prayer and how effective people feel it is; they also discussed the role prayer has in the lives of believers. Because of this focus, I instantly recalled my adolescence – specifically when I was twelve years old.

It was at this point in my life where my journey to adulthood began, and it did so without my permission. You may wonder,

"How can a child execute the responsibilities of an adult without first experiencing childhood?"

I always thought it was necessary to have time to live – to make mistakes and use the lessons from those mistakes to grow. I thought a person needed training, experience, and spiritual exposure to live as an adult in God's eyes.

But, at 12, I found myself asking, "What is happening to me? Why is my life taking this journey?" All I know is that I knew my life was different than my friends, and I knew it was because of God.

I'd developed a relationship with God at an early age. It was always a tenacious reader of self-improvement and spiritual literature. Of my siblings, I was the child that spent a great deal of time with a grandmother in the church. My mother said that even then I was seeking and analyzing my roles and place in God's house. I've always had a quest to know and do God's will. Although I understood it wouldn't be an easy task, I welcomed the challenge.

<u>Chapter Two</u>

The early life of a Christian usually starts with a lot of rituals that typically need fine tuning. So I went to Sunday School; participated in group projects; sang in the choir; served on the Usher Board, and had a strong prayer life. I did this, every Sunday in a service that ran all day. I even listened to the preacher's sermons.

I watched carefully in meetings how problems arose – sometimes never getting solved. I watched groups of families. I noticed how members dictated the successes and failures of the church. Contrary to the belief of many, I learned that church and politics do intermingle, and that problems occur because of this relationship.

The concept of church is sometimes comparable to that of a business in that they both encompass moments of petty behaviors – strategies and all. This observation is not intended as spiritual bashing; it is simply to say that what I learned was not what I originally understood church to be. Despite whatever problems arose, I always believed God to be the ultimate solution.

<u>Chapter Three</u>

While I'm learning and growing via this awakening, I also experience what at the age of 12, I considered a life-changing event.

She was only 42. It was a cold, blistering snow day, and ice would not melt right away. The sidewalks were like frozen lakes, but not reflective to the eye. Children would have seen this as an opportunity for fun, but I knew it was dangerous to walkers and drivers. She was very faithful, wanting to go to work for the benefits it provided her family. Yes, she had a husband that provided for her and their six children; people at times would count them spoiled. She counted it a blessing because she knew that God was the source of everything.

I talked with her each morning as she finished getting things together and organized for the day. My father would begin his journey out before us and my grandmother would awake so she could watch us leave for school. So we all had jobs to do.

The time had come for her to leave, and she put on her nice, warm gray wool coat. She placed her favorite red scarf around her neck. She was always a fashionista – feeling and looking good and excited about being a woman. I hugged and kissed her, told her to have a good day, and to wish me luck on my test. She told my siblings to be good as she finished her goodbyes.

I watched through the eyes of a child as she opened the doors and stepped outside. I heard the crunch of the salt my father had put down earlier that morning. Then I heard a light scream......and there she lay with her head on the step. I rushed to the door and told her not to move.

She was dazed, shaken and scared saying, "my heart". I yelled to someone to call 911, and then ran next door because it felt as though no one was coming fast enough. I enlisted my neighbor's help to get us to the hospital, which he gladly provided.

The doctors began working on her based on my concerns and description of how the situation occurred. I sat with my feet dangling in the emergency room. The smell, drama, and loud noises took me to a place so different than the sounds of my normal life.

I was trying so desperately to close out the noise, but add the shouts of "code blue" to the mix, and I became extremely anxious. I felt panic rise in me and tears stream down my face. Was my mother okay? Was she dead? I sat, twiddling my thumbs, as the worse thoughts ran through my mind.

Suddenly, a young doctor came my way. He sat with me to calm me and to explain what was happening. "Valerie, your mother is pretty sick. She has a bad bump on her head, but the trauma allowed us to identify some heart irregularities." Then he paused for a moment. "Is there an adult I can discuss this with?" he asked.

My father had been notified that he needed to return home, but his job was in the suburbs, and it would take time for him to make it to the hospital.

The doctor continued, "Your mother has what we call tachycardia, which basically means her heart beats too fast. We will need to keep her for further observation and treatment." He further explained that she would have to be registered, and a nurse would assist me until my father arrived.

I needed to see my mother first. I walked into her triage room; I was not prepared for what my eyes beheld. I was only 12 years old, and all I could think was "Mommy, please be alright."

The doctor again provided reassurance regarding my mother's condition. But, I wondered how he could be so certain. Did he know something that I didn't know?

I knew that prior to this, our family operated as a well-defined team for each other. I knew that my mother loved working, and now this would take that away from her. I knew that if she had a heart problem, my father would have to be prepared to take care of me, my siblings, my mother and my grandmother – a role that he'd never undertaken before. I knew that my mother would be miserable with the changes that these limitations presented. My head exploded day and night with all of the questions, concerns, pain and anguish.

Once my father made it to the hospital and I returned home, my grandmother consoled me and encouraged me to pray so that God could ease my pain. I was confused as to what I should say. How could I pose my thoughts and concerns in a way that He would understand me?

My grandmother told me of God's mercy and His ability to hear all those who prayed sincerely – regardless of age. So that night, once everyone was asleep, I talked to God. I asked Him to help prepare me for whatever my mother and father would experience. When I made that request, I was simply asking for strength as it pertained to coping with my mother's illness. But little did I know, there'd be much more along the way for which I was being prepared.

Chapter Four

I thought my mother's illness would be temporary; that she would take her medicine and be alright in a couple of days. However, a couple of days turned into a couple of months, and a couple of months turned into years. Her sickness extended throughout my adolescence into adulthood.

I went to hospitals off and on to visit her, worked full-time, and went to college, all the while trying to decide what to do with my own life. I didn't know what I was doing and many times I felt alone.

In October 2013, I decided to take a sabbatical from the church. This was the same church in which I'd grown up and received much of my spiritual education. But in addition to the peril that had become my life, the church was now in the middle of a merger.

We were merging with our sister church – same denomination, just two separate buildings. Decisions had to be made about how to continue our existence while preserving the history of our church. I'd been a part of this church all my life; my family were founding members. However, I knew if I planned to continue in my belief and spiritual growth, leaving was what I needed to do. It may seem ironic that I would leave the church to get stronger spiritually, but I had witnessed enough church politics to know how things would unfold.

Churches go through financial and employee situations much like Corporate America. The difference is that since the church is a spiritual entity, it must deal more effectively with its members as they participate and contribute to its survival. With all I was going through, I didn't feel like going through the rigmarole.

There comes a time when you have to take inventory of your life to know that what you're doing is for the right reasons. And, in my case, being done in the name of Jesus.

Sometimes, it was hard to believe He was there, but I knew that He hadn't abandoned me. I prayed and talked to Him, and began to understand that even in the midst of my confusion He loved me to the point that He didn't allow me to become lost. I made mistakes, but I believed no matter how great my anguish, human shame, guilt or uncertainty, God still prevailed in me.

It can become easy to rely on our education or experiences to try to explain situations. At times, we can even attribute medicine and the knowledge thereof as the be all and end all to life's solutions. Many articles, books, and talk shows discuss a variety of subjects trying to provide an answer. But I have found that God must be the constant in every equation. He connects our spiritual life to provide a healthier human life. I know that everyone has a choice of what to believe; the Bible has existed for a very long time, yet it is still highly debated. It provides clarity but because of choice it can serve as a point of conflict. I choose to believe that despite all of my hardships, God is and will always be present to guide me through.

Chapter Five

As time went by, I continued to reflect upon my life and its direction. I thought about my upbringing and the importance of my mother and grandmother as well as the influence of their roles in my life. Then I thought about life today, and how everything seems so drastically different. Roles have changed. Responsibilities have changed. I always believed that it was the job of parents to provide wisdom and guidance as it pertained to health, wealth, spirituality and morality.

But nowadays, what used to be the age group for parents – has now become the age of grandparents. And that class has become responsible for not just taking care of their children, but their children's children as well. Compound that with work and oftentimes being caregivers for their parents, and the pressure can be downright overwhelming.

Although I understand that each situation is unique, I believe that as a society we would benefit greatly if we returned to the morals of my day. I believe that if parents allowed their children to take accountability and raise the children they created instead of taking them on as their own responsibility, it would teach a more effective lesson. Otherwise, these young people will just continue having children, and it becomes the responsibility of the grandparent (and in many cases the Department of Children and Family Services) to handle this issue of displaced children. This situation typically results in added stress, dysfunctionality and even death.

While I don't have any children, I'm reminded of the cooperative behaviors of my mother and grandmother. How they served as a team – my grandmother supporting my parents' decisions – everyone playing an equal role in raising the family – our home, our church, our community was all one cohesive unit. But nowadays there appears to be a conflict, a disconnect even, with spiritual and personal beliefs so much that the associated anxieties hinder the decision-making processes.

Chapter Six

Now that you have taken inventory of your Christian walk, duties and overall responsibilities, how do you feel about the results? How do you begin to prioritize what you need and what you need to let go?

We ask ourselves, "Why am I in this position? Should I remain in it?" Many Christians have made positional choices willingly or by indirect force. We are not talking about someone actually beating you up, but about compulsion by a stronger need of the church to take on positions that are not your calling.

So, how do you get out and do it well? Let's point out the obvious; the church knows it is a difficult position to handle, so you may want to meet with your pastor to discuss your concerns. Additionally, you and the pastor can meet with the committee as a whole to discuss and evaluate the concerns that you have discussed.

Next, have a well thought-out plan to transition from the position. This will give the church time to train and appoint a new person. It is your duty to make it plain that it is your wish to keep the position as well as to use strategies that will negotiate paid or unpaid assistance to help with the workload and time to effectively learn and research the position.

Chapter Seven

Do you believe what you say?
Why do we say the things we say?
Are we or do we know how
ignorant or intelligent we sound
about what is being said?

When it comes to conversations
and evaluations of self, we can
easily cross the fine lines into
modifying the criteria to judge
oneself. We see others' mess
clearly, but not our own. We tend
to harden our hearts at times and
will only believe what we can feel

and that negates true analysis.

We have had conversations where we believe we are truly being honest with God and ourselves because we are supposed to be in His presence, but the truth is that some only believe what they can feel and see. They don't believe in revealing themselves even if they think for one moment that God is not truly listening. So, the question becomes do we keep asking, keep seeking, and keep knocking for His will or continue to govern by our own will?

I was sitting in Bible study thinking about how we use our bodies and spirit to meet our basic and complex life needs. The most common words that are consistently a part of our growth and renewal process were the following: movement, sensitivity, growth, and excretion.

Personally, these words have appeared most often during New Year's Resolution time. Movement in a sense of emotional growth, relationship growth and spiritual and intellectual growth. Growth in a sense of natural flow of time, life's physical and spiritual needs, the natural rhythm of each life's calendar in years expanding over ten year implementations.

In the final months of the year 2014, I was poised to embark on a journey to embrace my spiritual gifts. I was encouraged to give this journey a theme: Who and Where is the Person of Peace and Presences? I needed to look at some serious areas of commitment in my life governing the church, my needs and its needs.

The areas of repentance and faith, rest and work, relationships, priorities, ministries, prayer, life and peace. I needed a personal checkup and a self-checkup. What's the difference, you say? There is a big difference: my personal checkup focuses on making sure I am not becoming spiritually ingrown, and on checking on areas that may have become skewed; patterns, energy and misdirected responses to outside pressures.

My self-checkup focuses on making sure I was not moving by man's will, and was instead focusing on God's will. This is an area of great importance. It determines the origin of my gifts. I have to be clear that the life being breathed into me is God's own breath and not man's ideology to make it on others' labor and talents.

Chapter Eight

There are times in my life when I need to speak to God; sometimes I do it in a verbal prayer, other times, I write Him letters:

Dear God,

I've not written in a while; I haven't done much reflecting lately. I have thought a lot about trying to inventory my life and spiritual needs. I continue to struggle with thoughts, actions and spiritual needs. I have struggled with and against good and evil in all areas of my life. I have not read my scriptures enough to stay guarded and clear of my own thoughts that plague me. I think about my physical and spiritual needs and keeping them intact to be of service to others.

How do I then begin to ask for help in my Father? I have had many conversations with others whose shame and fear of shaming the Father prohibited them from asking others for help. I like to think that my prayer life is strong enough to ask for this help on their behalf. I don't believe it makes you weak; I believe it makes you true to your thoughts, feelings and your level of relationship with God when you ask Him the hard questions. After all, we know that He is all knowing, all-seeing and all-doing so He knows what is going on inside us as well.

My life in the church as always made clear that the believer is commanded to walk independently of adverse circumstances – God can move and out the earth as He desires. He can move the same way in you; Christians exhibit the same characteristics of goodness, kindness, support and strength.

The goal is to understand and cooperate with God so He can work within us to combat those things that affect us negatively. So, why do we act and seem so unclear about God and what He can do? Disorganized thoughts or attitude can cause us to forget about God. He is the One who is more than enough, so jump up, jump on board, and change your attitude.

On this particular Sunday, I began to listen, analyze and think about how God wants to answer, provide and support my prayers. Now let us be clear; there are days, weeks, months and years when staying positive in my walk has had its challenges. The positive days influence my Father's goals for me. Negativity distracts my Father's influences on goals for me. The incorporation and power of prayer based on John Wesley's teaching in the Methodist Church states that if we don't pray, God is limited by the how, why and lack of the way we pray.

Chapter Nine

Dear God,

Question: In the Garden of Eden, what did Eve and Adam do that was not satisfying to God concerning not walking in His sight?

We know this question usually turns a church, general Sunday School and Bible Study and public conversations into chaos. But, remember this is a view and consensus of the language and conversation heard by a variety of people. No one side is proven to be better than the other; the purpose is sometimes to enjoy the conversation of others' views, conversations and concerns surrounding the writings of the Bible. To take things one step or level further, they try to analyze the powerful thinking of the Heavenly Father.

Eve listened to someone other than God and Adam and ate the fruit. She exercised choice that is given to us freely, and went over the two main authorities in her world. Adam, being an authority in this kingdom, neglected his responsibilities, exercised the same choice as Eve, listened to others, ate the fruit and abandoned the Father's authority.

I believe this freedom of choice is

the same we exercise in our lives, but we tend to make everyone else accountable for it.

In the Garden of Eden, we say Eve was deceived, but Adam transgressed, so what caused the deception and transgression to happen in a place that is so provisionally and covenant available?

The consensus states that in the end, it was a covenant agreement with God that was destroyed. When Adam and Eve superseded their covenant with God, the established relationship of sovereignty was destroyed. To sum it up, this situation painted God as unrighteous and a liar, which led to the banishment of His children and the battle for our spirit. This was not going to be tolerated by the Father, man-image-dominion-laws of the garden and consequences.

Chapter Ten

The relentless pursuit for peace is not the biggest topic worldwide. Historically, in small villages and large cities the ongoing pursuit of peace was what we equated to happiness. Fast forward to 2014; its existence began to be re-evaluated. As of 2015 we continue to be on a never-ending journey of peace that equates to happiness, joy, and loving hearts.

To speak of peace, we must meet certain needs before we can even feel comfortable broaching such an intense topic. We must also take into account whether or not the situation contains economic stability, shelter and safety, ideas which have never been clearly defined by our own constitution.

When I think of conflict and peace, I see how households and families linger so long in their problems. First, the situations go on forever, they trickle into every household of families that are intertwined on a consistent basis. The children disagree on all levels, worthwhile OR petty. They are jealous, unappreciative, dwell in their own wants and needs, they bring all their problems for others to solve, and they think individuals are disposable.

Chapter Eleven

It is clinically, historically and observationally known that the Black, African and American individual is at times unclear on how to identify with their own culture, ethnicity and place in this society. An understanding of the determining factors of required knowledge of survival of your legacy is needed. How do we begin to walk through America's history with the little we understand about our own history?

Do we begin with the Civil War or do we begin with the Bible? I don't believe we knew that our history started so long ago, or that slavery and servitude began before the Declaration of Independence and the Civil War recordings. It began before the White man and the Black man met.

It began with us hurting us for a profit. Yes, the truth will make you free. It may be hard to believe but it has been going on throughout the world. We've been selling ourselves to various cultures around the world. I will use the reflection of Bible Study, independent research to expound on my thoughts about the things that I have been exposed to and how they are challenging my mind to be open and renewed to this historical journey. Now be mindful that this is my life experience and exposure. Your beliefs and ideas may and may not be different. It is not to take away from you and your understanding; it is a discussion between me, myself and God. Now if it helps you then let it be just that and not a situation to fight about and be angry, because in the end God can defend himself, research can be checked and verified, and personal thoughts, lives and experiences is up to individual interpretation.

Chapter Twelve

We are all aware of the horrors of slavery, the injustice to the Blacks, and the lack of recovery of their given life status. Now let's talk about what is really wrong in this country of milk and honey, forty acres and a mule. We need to determine where the hate came from and what it is all about. Who will be the first to say 'This is not right and I will not be a part of it'? Who will be the first to say 'I'm not sure why I'm doing what I'm doing.

I've gotten lost in the transition of lies, deceit and others' driven anger.' It is no secret that Black culture struggles with truth, dignity and loss of cultural roles concerning their own demise. It is also no secret that African Americans want to believe the struggle has improved. It is no secret that American continues to thrive through segregation, and not just with Blacks but with many other cultures and ethnicities.

The great melting pot has done more than melt peoples' body; it also melted their legacy, morality, spirituality and willingness to live in peace. What is wrong with a group of people than cannot see past skin? Are they that used to hate? There is no real, rational reason to dislike someone based off the color of their skin. The way they look, the way they talk, the way they build their families. What is the real reason someone hates? I believe it is their own insecurity. They don't feel they can be what they want so they put down others and misuse them, attempting to take away from what is expected of them in their own thoughts and life struggles.

There is also the theory of being unable to develop their own sense of self following the inappropriate behavior of others that raised them or exposed their erroneous views to them. God has given us choice and free will, but when it is tainted by choices of others, it becomes harder to choose between right and wrong because we haven't trusted the voice God placed in us.

When you ask people why they hate someone, various reasons come to light: they think they are better than others, they think the other person/people are/is inhuman, they stink, they are uneducated, they don't take care of their families, they're thieves, they are nappy-headed, they have too many babies, or they are always in jail are some common stereotypes.

Well, this is nothing new. There are other cultures that have had the same things said about them, but their hatred for African-Americans, Africans, and/or Blacks has been going on for too long and has become sickening, ridiculous and lacking validity. One thing is clear: you are not God, and those that hate are not the ones who determine our destiny or anyone else's destiny in this life. The energy being wasted in hating should be used to solve life problems and survive in this world.

<u>Chapter Thirteen</u>

I was looking at television one day, and of course wedding movies were being advertised. I was not surprised, but memories of my own wedding preparations came to mind. I did not get married that year, and have no regrets. I did notice that it brought about self-reflecting questions like "Am I ever getting married?" and "Do I really have to be married?"

This question is prevalent in some minds of Christian women

because of Biblical teachings (You are supposed to marry, have children and be a good wife), so let's look at some things that really hit the minds of married, widowed and single women. To this end, I interviewed 40 males and females in my family, friends, job and community that fit in one or more of the aforementioned categories.

I laughed so hard when talking to my interviewed parties about marriage. They discussed the good, the trials and the releases of their marriages. It was surprising to learn that if they had to do it over, marriage and children would not be part of their life's equation.

They would have done things differently and the key was that need to have peace that surpasses all understanding and not have to go to the grave to get it. I was in awe because I thought marriage was a completion component of life for us all because God was into family.

It is clear that we are creatures that desire the touch and need for each other, but how much need has taken a toll on the relationship. It was clearly stated by the control group that each family and living situation comes with a partnership of personalities that do not always mesh well together. It can be very mentally and physically charging on the individuals in charge of making the decisions, implementing the decisions, and assessing the decisions of living together as a unit.

The participants entered into

marriage with some key factors that should have made the marriage mesh. They didn't marry those with POTENTIAL marrying qualities. They had criteria such as whether or not the potential partner had a steady job and whether or not each of them wanted to blend and/or extend families. Moral and religious beliefs, educational pedigree, waiting to marry later in life or simply choosing to live together, and even the shifting public attitudes about marriage and its low success rate compared to the success rate of living together.

They were very open about children, considering those born and not yet born. They stated the concerns of boundaries being set appropriately for children outside the marriage. They were very open about finances, because the need for education and finances raised the issue of trust and discipline. The years or phases, as they call them, come with varying degrees of intensity. The loss of a child, the loss of a job, becoming caregivers to parents, incorrigible children.... the list of factors goes on and on. They express the love, but that love is challenged by things that are hard to rebound from, like infidelity.

Just in case you were wondering why this topic, it is because I have been thinking again about whether or not I want to get married. By 2017 I will be 50. Even though you can marry at any age, I will have to revisit this goal to see if I want it anymore. I am at a crossroads because the pickings are few these days. I have been very reflective about my past relationships and my current situation to focus on the reality of where I am at this point.

Chapter 14

I was reading my weekly "Get Unstuck, Be Unstoppable" by Valorie Burton. She had a journaling topic, Trigger Your Happiness with this One Habit. The article asked several questions: What do you want to feel this summer? What would enable that feeling? Who do you want to do something fun with?

This article was right on time, as I was looking forward to my summer vacation from teaching.

We have too much going on in education right now that my brain needs a break, refreshing, renewing and plain old downsizing; June isn't coming fast enough! So, let me think about the first question. I want to feel renewed, strong, encouraged in my spiritual walk on a new level.

The second question? Some spiritual retreat time to write and reflect on accomplishing my writing goals set earlier in the year.

The third question? Taking trips with friends and family to accomplish these goals. I want to visit my brother in California and my aunt in Louin, Mississippi. We are our own happiness makers, but it is good to set some goals to support what you are doing.

Some things can be done without a plan, but these are specifics that have been a top priority in my journey to happiness.

Chapter Fifteen

Once again I was reading my weekly topic from 'Get Unstuck, Be Unstoppable' by Valorie Burton. This week focused on making decisions that help define your peace. The journal question offered opportunities to reflect on the life of your spirituality and well-being. I began to consider the questions What decision am I hesitating about? Who am I trying to please? In my current situation, what would a bold and courageous decision look like?

Well, I can surely agree that there are decisions we all are hesitating about, but none more clear than getting rid of relationships that do not meet our defined boundaries of happiness, prosperity and peace of mind, body and spirit. I have thought a lot about all the relationships I engage in on a daily basis and have concluded that family and mates need to be dealt with first.

We feel because we are related to people that we have to be included in all aspects of their lives positive and negative, and I truly disagree with this. I have spoken about how God had made it His business to instruct us in not allowing negative and inappropriate behaviors to net our lives. We have not implemented this theory in a proper manner, because we feel that we are not being good people if we do not put up with ongoing physical, verbal, indirect and direct inappropriate behaviors by others close to us.

The Father has clearly defined that we are to be teachers to each other, our children and to the world as a whole. We are to make clear decisions from all the possible solutions that fit the scenario and provide what the pros and cons will look like. It is not healthy to sugar coat life experiences for friends and/or enemies to leave them in a delusional state and then fall apart when reality hits.

We may not want to hear the truth, but many things would run differently if we practice sharing

61

that truth more with both the ones we love and the ones we don't.

In my current situation, what would a bold and courageous decision look like? It would look like relief, calmness and peace prevailing. I would have lifted something that should not have been there in the first place because it was not part of me to begin with.

We have to be careful about what we bring into our lives and how we allow it to stay. We have to know what to expect from ourselves and make sure we are the joy makers of ourselves, and that we don't turn our lives over to someone else.

We have to understand that we can also make things more difficult than what they should be because we are afraid of being alone or of not having something that was not meant for us anyway. I look back on the theory of subtracting something or a percentage of some situation out of your life yearly. This is not a bad concept to use to evaluate what is really going on in our lives.

I have been looking at some spiritual changes and relationship changes that will impact my well-being for the future. At this point I have no regrets with the changes I am making. I seek resources and the Heavenly Father that understands those changes, as well as to find a balance to focus more on me and my needs and the needs of others.

I have also begun to provide more conversation that encourage the use of other resources to family members and mates so that they learn to handle their own outcomes and be better strategically to handle their stuff without destroying family and friend relationships.

No, this is not being selfish, but beginning to live longer, think more critically and implement so that situations are more win-win than more lose-lose in relationships that we engage in. No, it doesn't happen overnight, but consistency and truth will set the ongoing groundwork. It is not your job to carry the weight of the world; my God handles that.

However, being prepared to be a servant/teacher provided in a different structure provides tools and not the role of the fix-it person. The role and goal is to make independent, analytical, critical thinkers and survivors of trials and tribulations.

Chapter Sixteen

Think about it: What fear causes you to say "yes" when you really want to say "no"? Is it the loss of a relationship when submissiveness is not meeting the need of the dominant partner? Is it the loss of a job when you are not being a people pleaser to be noticed for skills and talents that help move the boss into a positive light with his competitors?

Is it wanting the love of a parent who doesn't know you are on the planet? Is it the inability to speak the language of communication to be enforced in saying no at the right time to the right situations? We have fallen victim to fear, or just the word "no" because we have confused our servitude with fixing the situation in front of us.

"No!" is clearly established as a word and in its job to do exactly what it says. It demands, stands, and creates the boundaries not to be used for others' needs that comprises our own needs to a point of fear. So, why do we continue to say yes to things although we have not taken care of those things we can't change, and are not our responsibility to change?

We can't control ourselves or others all the time. Separate what you need not to be put in a situation just to support others' needs that comprise your self-worth, integrity and emotional stability.

"No" and "Yes" are small words that pack powerful punches, but are easy to take down when determining how and what works for you in any situation. There are five steps that can be taken to minimize the effect of these words.

First, analyze the people that you are working with in fear and reflect on the possible causes of the fear. Second, determine if they are no and yes people and if you can do without them in those areas of fear. Third, find scriptures that allow you to effectively deal with the fear factor you are experiencing with the individuals you find it hard to say no to.

Fourth, start deciding how much time to engage with these individuals and whether or not they need to be with you when making key decisions. Finally, devise a no phase-out schedule that will allow you to say no to those individuals at least once a week, once bi-weekly or monthly, or until you have the strength to say no on a consistent basis and with no reservations about having decided to say no.

Chapter Seventeen

I have decided to spend some time in spiritual reflection, meditation and direction for the remainder of the year. Why is this needed? The spiritual time is a privileged and needed time for any person to reflect on their life in Christ, in the world, about their future and goal-setting for future spiritual renewing.

We have all at some point in our lives questioned what we are doing when learning and

connecting to the life with God. I
have spent a great deal of my life
in the church in various roles of
servitude and have come to a
point of needing direction in all
aspects of my life.

I know some say in a day and time
of cults, failing churches and
Christians who look more like the
world than like Christ, that this is
still important to an individual's
whole being. I come from a family
that is generationally loud,
boisterous and highly active.

I, on the other hand, always desire
quietness, thinking and reflecting. I
sought out the Cenacle to help me
in my journey to move toward a
great movement of the Holy Spirit
to help deepen the spiritual
connection to the Heavenly
Father. It will also ensure that my

goal-setting for the church, community, education and writing lives are all in focus and on one accord.

I am now 49 and close to being half a century old. I have always wondered how to be an effective Christian without growing weary in my duties. How can I live a fuller, happier life? They keys are not in fear, defeat and/or turmoil.

Do we know that the peace that surpasses all understanding doesn't require us to go to the grave? I will be reflecting on my journal thoughts to become a more effective Christian with keys – understanding my self-image and how it engages in every aspect of my life: developing the skills to renew, rebuild, revitalize happiness and creativity in my life;

structuring new ways of setting goals and specific techniques for achieving goals so that worldly and spiritual are more spiritually reflective: Connecting to all the influences of the higher power to govern my life to its full potential.